the essence of eeew

Rich Grudman

The Essence of EEEW
By Rich Grudman

ISBN: 978-0-9895820-0-1
Cover Design by Scarlett Rugers

www.facebook.com/essenceofeeew

This book is dedicated to Tina, Alex and Maya who encourage and inspire me. I love you. And to my friends who flap...
Long live the Yellow Toad!

Note to reader:
For enhanced enjoyment, please read this book aloud.

Contents:

The Essence of EEEW

Adventures In Stall Number Three

Someone left a present

inside stall number three.

A golden soup, a splattered mess,

left there just for me.

Not sure why they chose

to take on such a feat;

But pee-pee was a plenty

and all over the seat.

Toilet number one

was occupied for sure.

Ferocious farting bellowed,

from just behind the door.

And it was even worse

at toilet number two.

More than just the yellow,

this throne was drenched in poo.

I really had to go,

My bowels full beyond excess;

But the nastiness in front of me

was really quite a mess.

There was no paper anywhere,

I could not make it clean.

The only path in front of me,

was to somehow try to lean.

I strained to pop a squat,

my legs beside the bowl;

The rumbling in my belly

getting closer to my hole.

All at once it happened,

I started to explode;

My legs they lost their balance

and I slipped to the commode.

The sensation was disgusting,

wet all over me;

It really isn't pleasant

to sit in someone's pee.

The lesson of this story?

Let me tell you this...

Next time you use a restroom,

avoid the bowl of piss.

<u>Hmm...I Wonder?</u>

Scratch butt, sniff finger;

Never a dainty delight.

Why do I do it?

Bo

Just after sunup

I was walking the dog;

Awaiting the emergence

of his habitual log.

Bo was hunched over;

His back legs spread wide.

Expecting his business

to come out with a glide.

He sat there a minute;

His sphincter he flexed.

But nothing came out;

Bo was perplexed.

So he squeezed and he pushed

with utmost frustration.

Then he looked at me miserably,

"I've got constipation".

What could I do?

Bo's my best friend;

I knew that I had to

clean out his rear end.

I thought first that maybe

we should go back to the house;

But Bo wouldn't move;

he just moaned and he groused.

I bent down behind him,

more like a stoop;

Determined to help him

get rid of his poop.

I took out my bag,

put it over my finger;

Slipped it in softly

but still gave him a zinger.

Searching for sausage

deep in his rump;

Gently I pulled

on the end of a clump.

While I was working

I hit a small blip;

The bag I was using

gave way to a rip.

And when it came out

Bo gassed with a sputter;

My finger was covered

with his thick chocolate butter.

But Bo felt much better

and he gave me a kiss;

A dog owner's worst job

is proctologist.

A Pedicurist's Nightmare

Green muck on my toe;

A line wedged next to the nail.

Keep scooping, dig deep.

Silent Butt, Deadly

Sitting in her classroom

with a very subtle smile;

Miss Lucy dropped a silent bomb

that could be smelt a mile.

As the teacher of the class,

her hair tight in a bun;

It never dawned on anyone

that she was the one.

It was so musty and so tart,

it seemed to never leave;

All the little kiddies looked like

they might start to heave.

Miss Lucy asked the children

for someone to confess;

Knowing all the while

that no one would say yes.

Miss Lucy played an awful game,

one she thought a hoot;

Pretending it was someone else

when it was she who made that toot.

Miss Lucy thought it funny,

so she spewed some gas again;

This time near young Maddie

whose head began to spin.

Poor Maddie couldn't stand the tang

from the cutting of the cheese;

The scent it overpowered her

and brought her to her knees.

Her belly started bubbling,

her mouth it tasted icky;

She started burping up her lunch,

it came out rather quickly.

Miss Lucy couldn't take the sight

and started puking too;

Kids were gagging everywhere,

the floor heaped up with goo.

The stench of farts, the sight of barf,

the muddle in the class;

Miss Lucy never once again

thought of dropping ass.

Impressive dump

A lofty brown heap,

Rising above the water.

I'm three pounds lighter.

Booger Jar

It was arranged to look like

just an ordinary vase;

Sitting on a shelf at work,

an unassuming place.

It had no special features,

it had no special size.

It looked like decoration

to unsuspecting eyes.

But just within this covered jar

there was a secret stash;

An unusual collection,

a peculiar hidden cache.

Concealed inside this humble,

yet ornamental pot;

Resided an assortment

of old and dried up snot.

Billy Potter had his reasons,

an eccentric kind of guy;

He liked to store his boogers there

and have a large supply.

He used to try to keep them

in a spot behind his desk;

But sometimes they got dusty there

and he didn't like the mess.

Then he had a great idea,

as people sometimes do;

To keep his treasures in a jar

and keep them out of view.

Unearthing big and solid ones

would always make him smile;

And Billy had fun every day

adding to his pile.

He was also fond of slimly ones

that hang around and linger;

It gave him utmost pleasure

to watch them dripping from his finger.

He knew these would dehydrate

in a just day or two;

And didn't care what kind they were,

so long as the heap grew.

Just how people love their pets,

he loves those dried up clumps;

Every time he looks at them

it gives him big goose bumps.

It's funny that a booger jar

brings so much delight;

He thinks about it every day,

morning, noon and night.

No Such Yuck

Bird poop on my head.

A crappy day at the beach.

Lost the lotto too.

It's Always Something

As I walked through the door

from a two week vacation;

My senses were smacked by

an odd aberration.

There was something not right,

my nose was distraught;

My house stank like road kill

had been boiled in a pot.

Racing around

to discover the source;

I entered the kitchen

where the odor gained force.

At first I was only subject to the smell;

But when my eyes fell upon it,

they cringed promptly as well.

Laying before me

a small lump of flesh;

The remains of a house mouse

that was not very fresh.

Maggots were rampant

and dancing around;

Juicy grubs smiling,

erecting their town.

They ate through its fur

and they crawled through its head;

They picked and devoured

its eye to a shred;

Mouse entrails oozed

from the side of its belly;

A fly party gut bath

in white viscous jelly.

Those larvae were thriving

in putrefied meat;

My immediate mission

was to be their defeat.

So I cleaned up the carcass,

I scoured the floor;

The stench dissipated

as I finished my chore.

This was so unexpected,

a disturbing surprise;

An event I don't want

to repeat or reprise.

I called pest control

to douse and to spray;

Extermination is a service

I'm quite happy to pay.

<u>Nose Sewage</u>

Red, raw upper lip.

Into the ice cream, drip, drip.

Kids eat anything.

"Aaahhh...Sweet Relief"

In the car with no place to go;

Trapped in the middle lane,

when traffic got slow.

Cars all around

not showing a sign;

That movement was coming;

I was fenced in my line.

For two hours I sat there;

It was quarter past three;

Pretty soon I was thinking,

"I have to pee".

I sat in that spot

for two hours more;

My bladder was yelling now,

nearly a roar.

I wasn't sure what to do;

I was almost in pain;

I was going stir crazy

and I needed to drain.

I should have gone out

to the side of road;

Taken care of my business,

a stream would have flowed.

But the ache in my stomach,

I just couldn't think straight;

I saw a solution,

but it wasn't that great.

Right next to me

in the cup holder

Was the answer I thought of...

A bottle of soda.

The beverage was warm,

it was flat, it was old;

The cap it was missing

and the lip had some mold.

Inside was a gum wad

floating around;

It looked gross and decrepit,

and like it had drowned.

Another problem arose

as sometimes they do;

There was too much liquid already,

for me to add to.

Now that it's over

it's easy to think;

I should have opened the window

and poured out that drink.

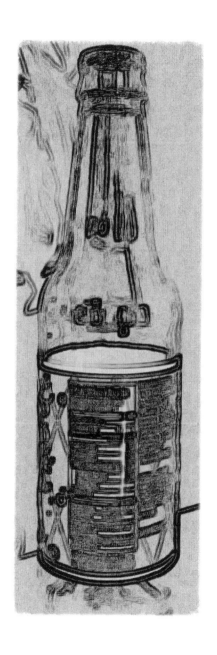

But like I have told you,

I wasn't clear in the head;

So what did I do,

I drank it instead.

That nasty foul soda

did not taste very good.

I did it for my bladder,

so my tongue understood.

Now the bottle was empty;

I was all in a scurry.

I had to go now

and I had to hurry.

I unzipped my pants

and pulled myself out;

I was doing my best

to take aim for the spout.

Again a small problem,

this time with the hole;

This game I was playing

called for real self-control.

Finally release,

it came out like a jet;

My hands were too shaky,

and well I got wet.

I wound up spraying

all over the place;

All over the dashboard

and even my face.

Then magically of course,

the traffic it cleared;

I was dripping and vulgar,

yet my bladder it cheered,

"Aaahhh...sweet relief!"

A Dutch Oven Is Inevitable

Under the covers,

taco meat vapor rising.

Need to share the smell.

Goober

Frankie stuck his finger

in a very holey place;

Intent upon extracting

the snot-ball in his face.

At the time of entry,

he encountered a surprise;

When the object meant to come out,

was pushed up toward his eyes.

Just like when you eat some food

that's just a tad too big;

Or drink a gulp of water

that's bigger than a swig.

Sometimes you cough, sometimes you choke,

sometimes you get it down;

Frankie snarfed that mucus orb

and chortled like a clown.

The gobby gloop it surfaced

in the back of Frankie's throat;

Almost like raw sewage

that gets dumped into a moat.

This gummy goober in his mouth

was the opposite of groovy;

The only thing that he could do

was to hock that loogie.

Good From Far, But Far From Good

I saw her from so far away;

My first thought was,

"Alright, Hey Hey."

She looked so good

and seemed so fine;

Her hair glistened

and her face shined.

She had the hips,

she had the moves;

She approached me

with her spicy groove.

I spoke first,

"So what's your name?"

Hoping I'd ignite a flame.

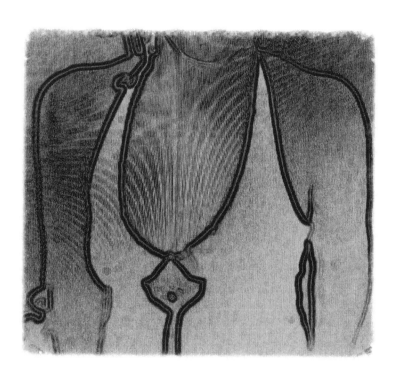

Then she smiled

and all went wrong;

Like on a game-show

when they sound a gong.

I could hardly move

from where I stood;

She was good from far,

but far from good.

Her teeth were twisted

and all bent;

My peepers screeched out

their dissent.

It was so unfair

and most obscene;

Those rotten chops

were unforeseen.

Her gums were swollen,

cherry red;

Decay was rampant

and widespread.

Some teeth were yellow,

some were black;

Most were putrid,

dipped in plaque.

Little nubs

ground to the core;

Impossible

to just ignore.

Those stubs were tiny

golden kernels

Truly vile, unjust,

infernal.

Fissures, pits,

a tooth abscess;

Her mouth was under

great distress.

I wasn't in

and with dismay

I said,

"No thank you, please go away"

What a disappointing evening;

A grotesque

and weird surprise.

I never saw it coming;

Her smile

our love's demise.

Just Like Nose Picking, Do It Alone.

Flaky, pasty wax;

Dead skin flecks itching like bugs.

Finger in the ear.

Always Opt For The Leather Seats

I was out for a drive

and was having a blast;

When my stomach first grumbled

with the pang of some gas.

I didn't think it a problem

as it's happened before;

So I leaned to the left

and let it out my back door.

But the grumbles kept coming;

They grew into a gripe;

Pretty soon things got hectic

at my exhaust pipe.

The situation had changed;

I'd come to a pass;

A bubble had formed

that seemed to have mass.

I considered the risks,

I opted to chance;

That this globule was gaseous

and wouldn't ruin my pants.

And so I expelled

what I thought was a puff;

But out came a dollop

of hot mushy stuff.

Like a doughnut that's filled

in the center with cream;

My cheeks were now stuffed

with a soft turd supreme.

It was wet; It was squishy;

It was sloppy and loose;

A regrettable place

to make number deuce.

My underwear flooded

with dirty brown sleet;

I attempted to keep my wet butt

off the seat.

I was worried the sludge

would somehow seep through;

Discolor the cloth,

leave a permanent view.

It was too hard to stand though,

while trying to steer;

So I had no choice,

but to sit on my rear.

I finally pulled over;

Leaping out of my chair;

Ready to scrutinize

my sodden state of affairs.

My slacks they were ruined

with a rather large spot;

And so was the seat cushion

which I scrubbed all for naught.

And so one more thought

that I'd like to impart;

If you pass gas beware

the mischievous shart.

Better Brown Bag It

Beware the wrath

of the plump lunch lady;

She may be smiling,

but her thoughts are shady.

Her name is Marge,

or Pat or Judy;

And whiny kids

have made her moody.

She serves the food up

with a smirk;

Today's special

is her dirty work.

She slips stuff in

between the cracks;

Like hair or bugs

or green ear wax.

Better watch

the "Sloppy Joes";

The secret spice

comes from her nose.

Forget about

the pizza sauce;

The chunks are morsels

from her morning floss.

And never ever

eat the beans;

They've touched the spoon

she never cleans.

This chowtime fare

is oh so gross;

You haven't eaten vomit,

but you have come close.

Oh why do you take

the chance each day?

Of eating

at this foul café?

Bring your lunch!

It's safe! It's sound!

And surely

not been on the ground.

It Starts With Just One

Joanie saw a cockroach

on the kitchen floor;

And she knew that when there's one,

there's always many more.

First thing first

she had to kill that interloper dead;

But she stomped her shoe a tad too slow;

It got away instead.

She opened up the cabinet

to try to find it quick;

Took a look way in the back

and thought she might be sick.

Swarming there among the pots,

an extraordinary sight;

An infestation of insects

she knew she had to smite.

Antennae feeling everywhere,

wriggling all around;

Big and brown with beady eyes,

some made a hissing sound.

Congregated near a clump

of old and moldy cheese;

Molting, eating, laying eggs

and doing what they please.

Good luck was on her side that day;

There was bug spray in the house.

She closed her eyes,

held her breath and gave the bugs a douse.

Roaches scuttled everywhere

as soon as they got wet;

Many dropped dead instantly

but there were some she didn't get.

Joanie swabbed the shelving clean,

wiping the remains;

Of many hundred cockroaches

And flushed them down the drain.

Some bugs were clever

and they hid deep inside the wall;

They'd come back another time

and next time they would sprawl.

Mouthwash: A Testimonial

Yesterday,

the wind bobbled over a field of

garbage

and gently uprooted some loose pieces

of soggy tissue over to the highway.

One particular bit

of mucus infused fabric

attached itself to my car

and travelled with me for twelve miles.

Then, near my street

the befoulment departed

and found a new home.

A little boy playing with a

yellow toad

picked up the excrement filled scrap

of used and abused paper

and for some ungodly reason

put it in his

mouth.

Bring On The Bleach

Hair bonds the grey sludge

That lives inside the sink drain.

Hock, spit, rinse and stink.

Nibble, Nibble, Gnaw

Chewing on fingernails

is a peculiar crass habit;

Munching ones cuticles

like a bunny does carrots.

An odd nervous tick

people do when they're bored;

As if eating dirt

is some kind of reward.

You wouldn't munch on a bowl

of gunk from your toes;

Or serve up for dinner

what comes out of your nose.

Eat lumps of dirt

or chomp dried up gum;

Or chew on a pen

that's been gnawed to and from?

So why do you snack

on the ends of your fingers?

Your skin gets so raw

and dirty germs linger.

Nails were not meant

for consuming at all;

Go buy a clipper

at just about any mall.

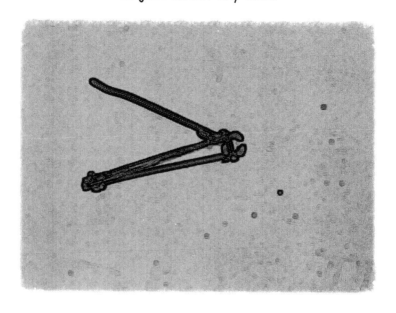

Stain

It really doesn't matter how

this caked on mess was splattered;

But anyway it's gonna be a job.

Black and tarry batter

is the essence of the matter;

And that will be the focus of my swab.

The pattern looks a lot,

like holes from a gunshot;

Clearly it came out with energy.

Dark and sprawling rot

and more than some, a lot;

Was clinging to the bowl proficiently.

Deep inside the basin,

my scrub brush starts to hasten;

Scouring the inside of the loo.

It feels like condemnation

to be scrubbing this damnation;

But someone has to clean out all this poo.

Pretty soon the deeds complete;

I even cleaned some off the seat;

The water nicely flushing down the drain.

I hope to never meet

these people who excrete,

So hard that they leave behind a stain.

.

<u>Loose</u>

Corn and tiny leaves,

Promptly squirting out of me.

Need to eat fiber.

If You Love Me You Will

My girlfriend was trying

some new toxin cleanse;

That was seen on TV

and confirmed by her friends.

She told me that it would be good

for my skin;

Improve my wellbeing,

help weight loss begin.

I was a skeptic

and I didn't think;

That too much would happen

from just drinking a drink.

So I smelled the concoction;

It looked like green swill;

She smiled her sweet smile and said,

"If you love me you will".

For two days I ate
nothing more than that juice;
I was starving and famished,
it felt like abuse.
But each time I felt hungry
and needed a shove;
My girlfriend so beautiful
reminded me of her love.

I finished that tonic
but instead of skin glow;
On my back formed a pimple
and boy did it grow.
It throbbed and annoyed me;
Its motive malign;
An infomercial success story
was not to be mine.

It matured very quickly

and produced a big head;

White pus in the center,

surrounded by red.

I did try to pop it;

But it was out of my reach;

My efforts were fruitless,

so the endeavor was ceased.

So I turned to my girlfriend,

I asked for her aid;

The pustule was beastly

and she looked dismayed.

She said,

"No way buddy, that thing makes me ill";

So I smiled my sweet smile and said,

"If you love me you will".

My logic convinced her,

she gave it a squeeze;

It popped and guck splattered

like an uncovered sneeze.

The secretion kept oozing,

chunks of white cream;

It gushed out of my backside,

a copious stream.

Just to be thorough

she gave one more pinch;

More toxins came out now,

more than an inch.

The hole in my back,

her hands filled with goo;

It may claim to be healthy,

but we bid cleansing adieu.

Get A Grip

Cool, wet, clammy hands;

Ever heard of a towel?

Soggy, flaccid, blech!

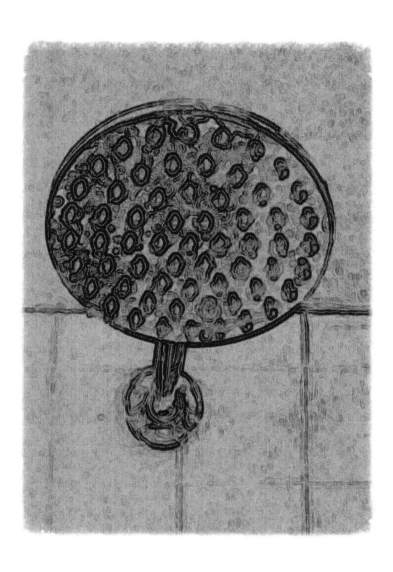

A Little TMI

Skid marks plagued the inside

of all of Barry's trunks;

And his rear was often packed

with tiny un-wiped chunks.

Barry was a tidy man;

But very, very hairy.

He always showered twice a day

to wash off the dingleberries.

Litter Box Lover

In the back of the house

when nobody sees;

Max the dog scrounges

with skilled expertise.

He rummages nuggets,

his favorite of treats;

That are left in the cat box

where Whiskers excretes.

He sniffs out the sludge balls,

a grubby affair;

And devours them quickly,

like a ravenous bear.

Sometimes they get trapped

in the hair of his beard;

He scampers about;

On the carpet they're smeared.

But what's worst is when

it appears that he's clean;

And people that pet him

overlook things not seen.

They allow Max to kiss them

all over the place;

Dispersing remnants of cat poop

on their lips and their face;

Some dogs prefer bacon,

others pork chops;

Max fancies treats

from a packed litter box.

So next time you see

happy Max with a grin;

Take heed to remember

where he likely has been.

The Essence Of EEEW

The County Fair was in town

and I went to play;

I rode many rides;

Ate a deep fried buffet.

I had meats; I had onions,

battered treats on a stick;

By the end of the day

I felt a tad sick.

My stomach was bloated,

it ached and it churned;

"Please give me relief!"

it cried and it yearned.

So I pressed through the crowds

as my belly grew knotty;

My eyes were ecstatic

to find a blue port-o-potty.

I hopped inside quickly,

turned around, locked the door;

Unleashed the foulness

and man did it pour.

More liquid than solid,

it burned and it singed;

Fire coo-coo some call it,

a consequence of my binge.

I sat there and squirted

my acid gruel slowly;

And tried not to think about

the stench most unholy.

Fair goers all day

adding to this ragu;

A fermented befoulment,

the true essence of eeew.

While I was sitting there,

in the midst of my purge;

An awareness arose;

A new mission emerged.

The lavatory that aided me

out of one caper;

Was mocking me now,

it was all out of paper.

I finished my business

and just pulled up my jeans;

But it wasn't that easy,

by any means.

I felt wet, foul and nasty,

burning and ripe;

The truth of the matter was

I needed a wipe.

So off came my pants,

my butt red and rare;

I dabbed and cleaned gently

with my good underwear.

A rag they became

as I finished the deed;

But I'll remember them always,

for sure, guaranteed.

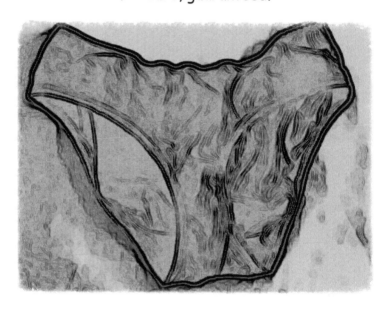

Scrubber

With popcorn in hand I entered the stands,

eager to see the next show;

I found me a seat and started to eat

when I noticed her in the next row.

She wasn't watching the screen,

but was busy it seemed,

holding her foot in her hand;

It was quite the commotion, watching the motion

of her grinding her callus to sand;

Dead skin was a-flaking;

Her hand it was shaking;

Working the side of her toe.

I almost got up and asked her to stop,

but just I couldn't make myself go.

Then she was rubbing;

No more like scrubbing;

What looked like the back of her heel.

The previews had started;

My eyes were contorted;

For me this whole thing was surreal.

The next thing I knew;

She blew and she blew;

Launching all of the shavings near me.

I was quick to discover

that my snack was now covered

in sort of a foot dust potpourri.

I should have walked out

or I should have got up;

I should have at least changed my seat.

Now my popcorn was wrecked

by her snowy skin flecks

and my night it was ruined by feet.

Tissueeew

I don't know why I have to,

but I need to know what;

Is remaining on the tissue

when I'm done wiping my butt.

Sometimes I notice color,

sometimes the little pieces;

But I just can't seem to look away

before I flush my feces.

The worst is when I feel like

I didn't get it with one swoop;

I toss aside the first wad

and get a second one to scoop.

Two tissue clumps all used up

and floating in the bowl;

Can really make me nervous

that they won't go down the hole.

Another thing I have to look at

before I throw away;

Is a hankie filled with mucous

and why I cannot say.

I always spread it open,

looking at the creamy goo;

Is it green and goopy?

Or is it clear white spew?

I know it sounds disgusting
but I just have to know;
What is coming out my openings
when I have to go.
There are worse things I can do,
than to take a little peek;
Touch it, smell it, taste it
would all make me a freak.

Deep Rooted

Over half an inch of
creamy guck
oozed out
like the first bite
into an éclair.

A tiny pop
sounded its final breath.
Soon the
protuberance
that ensnared the eyes
of onlookers,
who desperately failed
to turn away,
will be forgotten.

Except by its cousin
who lives amongst the filth left behind.
Pimple poppers beware!
Oh the
vengeance
of the angry zit!

Keep Your Shirt On, Will Ya?

One large coffee mole

with a single hair yelling,

"Check me out baby!"

Wipe Off And Go

My corned beef sandwich
was piled so high;
A thin layer of mustard
on sour rye.
A plate full of pickles,
a dish full of fries;
My stomach was singing
and so were my eyes.

It looked so delectable;
The smell gave me pleasure;
So I took a big bite
and bit into a treasure.
It was moist, it was juicy,
the flavor was bright;
But then my tongue detected
something not right.

My dinner that started

off with such flair;

Had been interrupted

by a menacing hair.

My fingers were searching

to find an end;

Hoping to take out

this villainous friend.

I was trying to salvage

the rest of the meal;

But the intruder was squirmy

much like an eel.

In a mouthful of meat

that was partially chewed,

I fumbled around

but that strand was quite rude.

I started to tug

on that thin lanky rope;

Hoping to yank it out

with one stroke.

I pulled and I pulled

and I pulled and it snapped,

leaving most of its body

in my mouth trapped.

Recouping had failed,

it was time to vacate;

So I spit out that mush meat

onto my plate.

It landed on top

of my fries with a plop

and looked like a bundle

of pink gooey glop.

But I still needed to eat

as I was famished

and nothing was wrong

with the rest of the sandwich.

So just to be safe

I took off the bread,

where I found more blonde locks

from the waitress's head.

At first I was mad,

this was revolting;

I could hardly believe

what my eyes were beholding.

But then I thought, "Wait,

this isn't too bad";

Remember the rule,

and deliciousness will be had.

So that's what I did;

And just so you know,

my rule for eating is

wipe off and go.

<u>Particles</u>

You can't see them but they're there,
lurking.
Persevering and resolute;
Miniscule scraps of excreta,
meant to be flushed away
wait like surfers for the perfect wave.
When they get the chance
they catch the air,
leaping playfully.
The funnel comes
and up they go.
You may not know it but the door is open.
You've let them in.
They're invited to a secret party
hosted on your bathroom vanity.
They congregate festively,
Dancing and swirling,
feasting in revelry.
Relishing the opportunity to celebrate
prolonged life.
All upon the bristles
of your slightly moist
and minty
toothbrush.

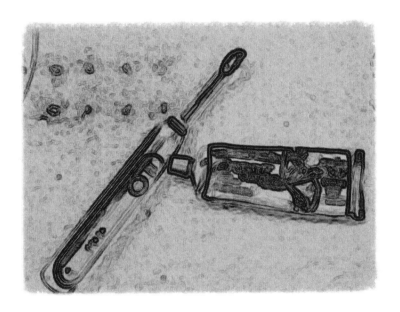

Utterly Empty

Digestively speaking

it was not a great day;

A monster was in me

who was up to foul play.

At making me woozy

he was an over achiever;

I was feeling quite sick,

a regular heaver.

My forehead was hot

with fever ablaze;

My belly was aching

with raucous malaise.

Five cookie-tosses already,

my stomach in pain;

It was hard to imagine

there was much left to drain.

But yet one more time

I felt a bit queasy;

So I ran to the toilet

hoping it would come easy.

I gagged and I choked,

blood rushed to my head;

My throat was so raw,

it wished I was dead.

I doubled over the bowl,

hocking up phlegm;

It dribbled out slowly;

then the spasms began.

A first a deep belch

that tasted most vile;

Followed up with a serving

of noxious green bile.

It bubbled into my mouth,

burning my tongue;

Its essence like marinade

of venomous dung.

I spit and I sputtered

and wiped off my lips,

My head was all sweaty

and covered with drips.

I flushed the remains

and I stood up to leave;

Then the feeling came back

and I began to dry heave.

The burping and aftertaste

of putrefied rot;

Endless sweating and cramping,

and all for squat.

My body kept thinking

it's time to throw up;

But nothing was left

for me to upchuck.

I just sat there and waited

to get rid of the urge;

Utterly empty

with nothing to purge.

<u>Winner</u>

The surprising part about it

was not the sound or smell or spittle;

But that belcher acted like

she was granted an acquittal.

Joan was a financial whiz,

a woman of esteem;

A mucky-muck by any measure

in the company regime.

She let one out right in Roy's face

with the force of a light breeze;

He could clearly taste the garlic fries

and perhaps a hint of cheese.

He wiped some droplets off his cheek

and expected her to say;

How embarrassed that she was,

that she'd make it up to him some way.

But Joan just stood there,

carried on as if it never happened;

Roy was sort of flabbergasted

by her course of action.

He was an accounting guy,

a problem solving sleuth;

He knew that this predicament

called for actions most uncouth.

He learned a trick to swallow air

when he was a boy;

He wriggled up his diaphragm,

preparing to deploy.

From deep within his lower bowels,

his decomposing lunch;

Hot dogs, pickles, raw onions,

would surely leave a punch.

The gas assembled rapidly,

swirling up his gullet;

He cocked his head and spit it out

like a large exploding bullet.

The stench was raw, the blast was loud,

a deep staccato sound;

The vapor smacked her brutally,

nearly knocked her to the ground.

It stung her eyes,

the acrid smell of disintegrating meat;

A spicy and a pungent stink

like the tang from sweaty feet.

At last Joan said,

"We're even, please,

I can't take it anymore."

Roy just smiled and said "okay",

he'd won the burping war.

Poop Talk (A Haikeeew In Reverse)

Some people call it doody,

Others call it stool.

All this fecal talk is crap.

Further Accounts Of Stall Number Three

I was taking care of business

inside stall number one;

The flatulence ferocious,

as if my guts had come undone.

When I heard somebody race in

to use toilet number three.

I knew they'd have a problem there,

it was soaked and full of pee.

Also, I just took the paper

and it was the last roll;

So I couldn't help but feel bad

thinking how they'd use *that* bowl.

Then my belly made a funny noise,

Like a very sloppy slurp;

Followed by a murky blast,

a boisterous backside burp.

I sat there farting endlessly,

waiting for brown stuff;

But it never made it out of me;

It was a vaporific bluff.

So I never used the tissue;

But I'm glad I made the score;

Because a urine filled calamity

was just behind the door.

ABOUT THE AUTHOR

Rich is an amusing man;

He thought this book up on the can.

He has a job, two kids, a wife.

He lives a rather normal life.

So if you're wondering, "Why, Why, Why?"

Think back a bit to Junior High.

He wrote this for himself he did;

It makes him feel just like a kid.

For even more, please take a look,

Essence of EEEW is on Facebook.

www.facebook.com/essenceofeeew

28345999R00062

Made in the USA
Charleston, SC
07 April 2014